Dedication

To Kenneth, Christine, and Kevin, and to the wonderful students I have worked with who have been instrumental in helping me develop this program.

Scholastic Inc. grants teachers permission to photocopy the reproducible pages from this book for classroom use. No other part of this publication may be reproduced in whole or in part, or stored in a retrieval system, or transmitted in any form or by any means, electronic, mechanical, photocopying, recording, or otherwise, without written permission of the publisher. For information regarding permission, write to Scholastic Inc., 557 Broadway, New York, NY 10012.

Cover design by Norma Ortiz

Interior design by Ellen Matlach Hassell for Boultinghouse & Boultinghouse, Inc.

Cover and interior illustrations by James Graham Hale, except page 2 by Maxie Chambliss

ISBN 0-439-17898-3

Copyright © 2002 by Veronica Robillard. All rights reserved.

Printed in the U.S.A.

1 2 3 4 5 6 7 8 9 10   40   09 08 07 06 05 04 03 02

Contents

Introduction 4
Getting Started With Write & Read Books 5
Reproducible Letter to Families 18

Month-by-Month Write & Read Books

Suenan las campanas SEPTIEMBRE 19
Otoño SEPTIEMBRE 23
La cosecha del otoño OCTUBRE 27
Manzanas, manzanas OCTUBRE 31
La arañita NOVIEMBRE 37
Doy gracias NOVIEMBRE 41
Una fría mañana de nieve DICIEMBRE 46
Cómo hacer un muñeco de nieve ENERO 53
¡Es divertido contar hasta cien! FEBRERO 58
Si yo fuera presidente FEBRERO 65
Feliz día de San Valentín FEBRERO 69
¿De qué tamaño es un duende? MARZO 75
Los colores de la Tierra ABRIL 80
¡Es primavera! MAYO 85
Mi libro de recuerdos JUNIO 89

Reproducible About the Author Page 94
Reproducible Write & Read Book Templates 95

Introduction

Write & Read Books are a creative and interactive way to teach early literacy skills to children! The first Write & Read book was so well received that I have developed a second book in the series. *Month-by-Month Spanish Write & Read Books* takes you through the school year with topics such as back to school, seasons, special events, holidays, and more! Using the predictable, patterned story templates, children write and illustrate their own books, which they can then take home and share. Children learn by writing, reading, listening, and speaking. They also learn from the feedback and support of their audience.

As they create their own unique books, children experience success and a sense of ownership. They realize that they can do the writing and the reading. The process is self-nourishing. As children develop confidence, they are motivated to write more and to read what they have written.

The books are both easy to make and easy to use. I usually make a model of each book and share it with the class as I introduce the concept. You'll find suggestions for presenting individual books on pages 5–17. You may want to reproduce the "About the Author" template on page 94 to add to each book.

Children complete the books in keeping with their own literacy development. The amount of direction and instruction depends on children's needs. Preliminary group work on the chalkboard or chart pads is often helpful to get them started. For early learners, I sometimes make dotted-line letters or write letters in fine yellow marker as children dictate the words for their stories. For advanced learners, I encourage a more colorful and detailed text. Illustrating the stories provides children with another way to express their ideas.

The amount of time and the depth of the lessons for each book vary. I encourage you to extend the concepts and ideas to the degree that time, resources, and student needs allow. However you decide to use Write & Read Books, you'll find that they are easy to integrate into your teaching.

A critical component is to provide children with the opportunity and encouragement to read their books again and again—to themselves, to other students, to family members, or to other classes. As they share their books, children learn to use cues such as patterns in the text, high-frequency words, and illustrations to help them become fluent readers.

Each book includes a "Comentarios" page on the back cover. This page provides a place for family members or classmates to respond to, and to reinforce, the author's efforts with positive comments. You'll find a letter to family members on page 18, which you can duplicate and send home, explaining the importance of this feedback in helping children grow as writers and readers.

I suggest considering a predictable pattern in making and sharing the books. I include them as part of my scheduled routine. We make a book in class each week. Children take their books home every Friday and return them on Monday with responses from family members.

In addition to making the 15 books included here, you and your class may want to write your own stories. Use the templates on pages 95–96 for students' original work.

With Write & Read Books, children, teachers, and parents all join together to foster literacy growth. I think you'll find the experience both rewarding and enjoyable.

Getting Started With Write & Read Books

When introducing a mini-book, it is beneficial to create a completed sample to show the class. By reading through your book and pointing out all the steps you took, you help children feel comfortable when they create their own mini-books.

The books have been designed for ease of assembly. See the detailed instructions below. It is best to assemble the books together as a class. Of course, you might want to assemble the books yourself, depending on the time of year and the level of children.

Assembling the Books

1. Copy the pages for books on standard 8½-inch by 11-inch paper, making the pages single-sided.
2. Fold the front cover/back cover in half along the dashed line, keeping the fold to the left side.
3. Fold each inner page in half, keeping the fold to the right side.
4. Place the inner pages inside the cover and staple three times along the spine.

Suenan las campanas

SEPTEMBER pages 19–22

Purpose
Children focus on the transition from summer to the school year. Children review school-related vocabulary.

Strategies for Starting
Talk about the changes from summer vacation to back-to-school routines. Ask: *What was different in your home this morning compared to mornings in the summer? Was there a difference in your after-dinner activities last night compared with before school started? Was your bedtime last night earlier or later than your bedtime before school started? Did you feel different this morning than in the summer?* Invite children to note what else has changed or not changed in their daily routine and lifestyle. Perhaps make a chart comparing things that are different and things that are the same.

Introduce the Book
Display the model book that you made. Read it aloud to the class. Explore other possibilities for filling in the missing words. You may want to brainstorm as a group a list of possible responses for each page. Write children's ideas on the board for children to refer to as they make their books.

Encourage children to personalize their books according to their feelings about the start of the school year.

Make the Book
Duplicate and pass out pages 19–22 of this book. Either preassemble the books or help children assemble their books. Stress the importance of drawing illustrations that match the text. Remind children to include their names on the cover. Refer to the introduction for suggestions on how to support children who need extra help.

Share the Book
Invite children to take turns reading their books aloud to the class. Encourage one-to-one word correspondence. Send the books home along with the letter on page 18. When children return their books, add them to a back-to-school display. The names printed on the front covers will allow children to become familiar with the spelling of one another's names.

Beyond the Book
You may choose to elaborate on these topics:
- comparing and contrasting (lo que más me gusta/lo que menos me gusta)
- deciding what makes something special

TEACHING TIP: This book is a great way to get to know about your students at the start of the school year!

Otoño

SEPTEMBER pages 23–26

Purpose
Children observe the seasonal changes of autumn.

Strategies for Starting
Talk about the leaves changing color and make a list of autumn color words. Encourage seasonal awareness by asking: *What are the four seasons? What season is it now? What are some of the special features of autumn? What are some of the changes that we observe? What do you like about autumn?*

Introduce the Book
Display the model book you have made. As you read it aloud, emphasize the phrase "Veo ____." Let children guess the ends of sentences based on the illustrations. Discuss the meaning of the words *observar* and *observación*. Explain that children will observe the changes that take place during autumn and will record their observations in their books.

Make the Book
Duplicate and distribute pages 23–26 of this book. Either preassemble the books or help children assemble their books. Discuss the relationship of pictures to print. Explain that pictures can be valuable clues to figuring out words. To demonstrate this idea, you could compare a picture book without words and a picture book with simple text and rich illustrations. Explain that the words children write in their books should match the pictures. Invite children to draw a picture of themselves on the cover. On the last page, have them illustrate their favorite part of autumn.

Share the Book
Invite children to share their favorite pages of their books with the class. Send the books home for children to read to family members.

Beyond the Book
Develop children's understanding of autumn by exploring changes in daylight hours and temperature. Compare and contrast earlier to later, warmer to cooler, and so on. Discuss special activities or celebrations that take place in autumn.

TEACHING TIP: Develop an autumn word bank for use in different kinds of writing, such as journals, creative writing, poetry, and scientific exploration. You can then compile student work for a class book about autumn. Try making a book for each season!

La cosecha del otoño

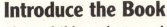

OCTOBER   pages 27–30

Purpose
Children learn about the fall harvest in a patterned, predictable text. Children review vocabulary related to the harvest. Children support text with illustrations.

Strategies for Starting
As a group, brainstorm a list of foods children like to eat in the fall. Then discuss what foods they like to eat during other seasons. Are they different or the same? Ask: *Why might you prefer different foods during different times of the year?* Then discuss how we get our food, especially food that is harvested. Ask: *Who grows fruits, vegetables, and grains? How do they grow it? How does it get to us?*

Introduce the Book
Show children the sample book that you have made. Read aloud the first few pages. Invite children to follow the pattern and join in after you have read the first line of each verse. Repeat until they are familiar with the pattern. Point out the phrase "en el/la _____." Have children locate that phrase on each page.

Make the Book
Duplicate and pass out pages 27–30 of this book. Either preassemble the books or help students assemble their books. Review the relationship of pictures to print. Point out that students can use clues in the text to help them draw their pictures. On the last page, they can fill the shopping cart with food.

Share the Book
Divide your class into six groups and assign each group a verse. Ask each group to make up a movement to represent the action (or verb) in the verse. Give children time to practice reciting their verse with movement. Then have the groups read their verses in the order of the book, acting out the verbs. Next have the class read the entire book together, with everyone doing all of the movements. Finally, send the books home for children to share with family members.

Beyond the Book
- Make an audiotape recording of students reading the book together. Keep it in a listening center with students' books.
- Make labels for objects in the classroom using the phrase "en el/la _____" (examples: en la cesta, en el armario, en el cesto de la basura).
- Use the book to introduce a unit on farms and harvesting.

TEACHING TIP: Invite students to make up their own verses following the book's pattern. Then ask them to add illustrations that support the text. Compile students' work into a class book and ask each student to share his or her page with the class.

Manzanas, manzanas

OCTOBER   pages 31–36

Purpose
Children review numbers. Children practice counting backward in a patterned text. Children practice simple subtraction.

Strategies for Starting
Review the numbers 0 to 10. As a group, practice counting backwards from 10 to 1, like a rocket countdown. To introduce subtraction, display a group of ten apples (or other objects) in the front of the room. As the class counts backward, remove one apple at a time so that students can see the pile getting smaller.

Introduce the Book
Show children your sample book. Read aloud the first few pages. Invite children to follow the pattern and join in after you read the first line of each page. Then read the book in unison, emphasizing one-to-one word correspondence.

Make the Book
Duplicate and pass out pages 31–36 of this book. Either preassemble the books or help students assemble their books. Ask students to draw the appropriate number of apples in the tree on each page. (For example, students would draw 8 apples for "En un árbol hay ocho manzanas.") Then show students how they can cover up one apple and count the other apples to solve the subtraction problem. Point out the lines where they can write their answers. Remind them to write their names on the front covers.

Share the Book
Invite children to read the book in unison. Children may also read the book in pairs, alternating pages. They can use manipulatives while they read to reinforce the concept of subtraction. Have them take their books home to share and get responses from family members.

Beyond the Book
- Study connections between numerals and number words.
- Discuss the use of the question mark and ask students to make up their own sentences using question marks. Demonstrate how a sentence sounds different if it ends in a question mark. Ask them to read their sentences with a questioning intonation.

TEACHING TIP: Use **Manzanas, manzanas** to connect with math lessons such as subtraction, more/less, and counting backward. Try making up a similar rhyme in which other objects are added or subtracted. Have children suggest different objects and numbers to complete the rhyme.

La arañita

NOVEMBER pages 37–40

Purpose
Children identify direct quotations. Children identify descriptive words (adjectives).

Strategies for Starting
Ask children where they might find a spider in their homes. Discuss how and why spiders make webs.

Introduce the Book
Share the model book that you made. As you read aloud, give the spider a distinct voice so that students can hear the direct quotations.

Make the Book
Duplicate and pass out pages 37–40 of this book. Either preassemble the books or help students assemble their books. Review the relationship of pictures to print. Ask students to find what the spider says on each page by looking for words inside the dashes. Then have them copy the quotations into the talk balloons to reinforce the concept. Invite students to draw a picture of themselves on the last page with the spider.

Share the Book
Assign children roles from the book as the different animals and the spider. Encourage children to act out the descriptions of the animals as other students read aloud. For example, the student playing the goat should act grumpy. Then send books home for children to share with family members.

Beyond the Book
Introduce adjectives as words that describe people, places, or things. Read the book again, stopping to ask students to describe the animal the spider meets on each page. For example, ask: *What kind of goat did he meet?* (una cabra *gruñona*) and *What kind of child did he meet?* (un niño *alegre*) Explain that these words are adjectives. Ask students to think of adjectives that describe other animals beginning with the same letter, such as *un perro pequeño* or *una mariposa maravillosa*. List on the board the adjectives they think of. Challenge the class to come up with an adjective and animal for every letter of the alphabet. Then have each student illustrate one animal/adjective combination for a class "animal, adjective, alphabet" book.

TEACHING TIP: Make a spider learning center with books and posters about spiders. Encourage children to write creative stories or reports about spiders; draw or paint spiders using photographs for reference; and create three-dimensional spiders using pipe cleaners, paper rolled into balls, and other materials.

Doy gracias

NOVEMBER pages 41–45

Purpose
Children identify what they are thankful for in their lives.

Strategies for Starting
Discuss what it means to be thankful. Invite children to share what they are thankful for. Point out that we sometimes take things for granted and it is good to think about the gifts or blessings in our lives. You may want to connect this book with the celebration of Thanksgiving.

Introduce the Book
Display the model book that you made. Read it aloud to the class. Point out that the sentences begin the same way. Stress one-to-one word correspondence. Explain that the pictures you drew are helpful clues to recognizing the other words on each page.

Make the Book
Duplicate and pass out pages 41–45 of this book. Either preassemble the books or help children assemble their books. Invite children to draw a picture of themselves on the cover with something for which they are thankful. Elicit possible responses for each page. Write these on the chalkboard to help children with spelling and vocabulary development. Stress the importance of drawing pictures that support what they have written.

Share the Book
Emphasize that the sentences have a patterned beginning. Invite children to share their books with a partner. Ask for several volunteers to read their books aloud and to share their pictures with the class. Have children bring their books home to read to family members over the Thanksgiving holiday.

Beyond the Book
- Make a bulletin board display featuring a large turkey with colorful cut-out feathers. Have each child create a "feather" for the turkey with the words "Doy gracias por _____." Encourage them to fill in the blank with an idea from their book.
- Make a class graph of students' favorite Thanksgiving foods.

Una fría mañana de nieve
DECEMBER   pages 46–52

Purpose
Children count objects and write numerals. Children review verbs. Children review characteristics of winter.

Strategies for Starting
Invite children to share observations they might make on a cold, snowy winter day while on their way to school. Whisper different verbs for children to act out, such as *estornudar, bailar, saltar, llorar, y reir.* Ask other children to guess the verb being acted out.

Introduce the Book
Read aloud the sample book that you made, emphasizing the verbs. You can let children take turns counting the number of objects on each page.

Make the Book
Duplicate and pass out pages 46–52 of this book. Either preassemble the books or help children assemble their books. Have children count the number of objects on each page and write a numeral on the blank. On the last page, children can draw a snowy winter scene. Then invite them to color in their books and write their names on the covers.

Share the Book
Have children practice reading their books with expression to a partner. Then ask pairs of partners to identify all of the verbs. Invite volunteers to read the book (or parts of the book) expressively while the class acts out the verbs. Send home the books for sharing with family members. When the books are returned, they can be added to a winter display.

Beyond the Book
- Ask children to identify the adjectives in the book. Ask: *What kind of snowflakes were falling? What kind of icicles were hanging?* This patterned questioning will help children find the adjectives on their own. Make a list of the adjectives from the book, then have children generate their own adjectives to add to the list.
- Using the templates on pages 95–96, have children work collaboratively to create similar books with titles such as *Una escuela elemental feliz*.

Cómo hacer un muñeco de nieve

JANUARY   pages 53–57

Purpose
Children count objects and write numerals. Children recognize sequence words *(primero, después, por fin)*.

Strategies for Starting
Have children share their experiences with making snowmen. Encourage children to describe the process of building a snowman. Ask children how they would teach a younger friend or sibling to build a snowman, step by step.

Introduce the Book
Display the book that you made as a model. Also emphasize the importance of using clues in the illustrations to help students fill in the appropriate text.

Make the Book
Duplicate and pass out pages 53–57 of this book. Either preassemble the books or help children assemble their books. On page 1, students can draw themselves building a snowman. On pages 2–7, have children count the objects on each page and fill in numerals on the appropriate lines. Finally, invite children to color in the pictures and add details to personalize it. Suggest that on each page they draw themselves building the snowman.

Share the Book
Ask for volunteers to read pages of the book while other students act out what is being read. Send the books home for students to read to family members.

Beyond the Book
- Invite children to write or tell a short story using sequence words. (The story can be their own or one they already know.) You might give them suggestions to start the story, such as "Hubo una vez . . ." or "Lo primero que sucedió . . ."
- Ask children to use sequence words as they write or tell instructions for a task that they are experts in, such as making a peanut butter and jelly sandwich or doing a cartwheel.

¡Es divertido contar hasta cien!

FEBRUARY pages 58–64

Purpose
Children draw 100 objects in ten groups of ten. Children review opposites.

Strategies for Starting
Have students think about how many days they have been in school this year. Review counting to 100 by 10's, 5's, 2's, and 1's. Ask students to think of combinations that equal 100, such as 50 + 50, 99 + 1, and 25 + 25 + 25 + 25. Have them consider how many hundreds, tens, and ones are in 100.

Introduce the Book
Share with the class the sample book that you made. Encourage children to note the correspondence between your drawings and the text. Discuss the concept of opposites and have children generate a list of opposites.

Make the Book
Duplicate and distribute the book. Either pre-assemble the books or help children assemble their books. Discuss what things are hot, cold, big, small, round, square, soft, hard, loud, and quiet. List them on the board for children to refer to as they make their books. Have children draw ten pictures in each category. You may ask them to complete a section of the book each day for several days.

Share the Book
Share and compare the finished books as part of your 100th Day celebration. Send the books home for students to read to family members and friends. When they return the books, display them on a bulletin board titled "¡Celebra 100!" before adding them to students' personal libraries.

Beyond the Book
Explore the numbers 1 to 100 with activities in writing, reading, science, math, social studies, art, music, and physical education. Here are some ideas:

- Count 100 kernels of popcorn; then pop and enjoy!
- String 100 pieces of cereal to make a necklace.
- Make a headband with 100 tally marks on it.
- Make student badges that say "¡Llevo 100 días en _____ grado!"
- Count 100 steps.
- Read 100 books.
- Graph the colors of 100 colored cubes.
- Make a chart with 100 thumb prints.
- Count 100 raisins; make groups of 2, 5, and 10 before eating!
- Count 100 cents.
- Do 100 math problems.
- Spend an imaginary 100 dollars.
- Sort 100 shells, buttons, beans, or other small objects.
- Write a story with 100 words.
- Make a design or picture with 100 toothpicks.
- Make a list of 100 words students can read.
- Display collections of 100 objects.

Si yo fuera presidente

FEBRUARY pages 65–68

Purpose
Children imagine themselves in the role of President.

Strategies for Starting
Invite children to share their knowledge of the presidency. Discuss where the President lives and what the President does. Have a discussion about what it would be like if they were President and what they would do in that role. Encourage students to use the correct verb tense, "Si yo fuera presidente, yo haría . . ."

Introduce the Book
Display the book you made as a model. Ask what the title *Si yo fuera presidente* means.

Make the Book
Duplicate and pass out pages 65–68 of this book. Either preassemble the books or help children assemble their books. You may want to brainstorm possible responses as a group to help children develop their ideas. Write students' ideas on the board for them to refer to as they make their books. Encourage children to draw pictures that support what they have written. Suggest that they draw themselves sitting behind the desk on the cover.

Share the Book
Invite students to share their books with partners or with the class. Ask them to respond to their peers' work with thoughtful questions or positive comments. You may want to model this with examples such as, "I like the way you said that if you were President you would make peace all over the world," or "How would you reach your goal of helping people get enough food?" Send the books home for students to read to family members and friends.

Beyond the Book
This book can be readily connected with Presidents' Day and a unit on the presidency. Make a bulletin board display featuring famous presidents such as Abraham Lincoln and George Washington, as well as the current president and recent presidents students recognize. Display students' books alongside the pictures.

TEACHING TIP: Use this book as a springboard to discuss other careers. Ask students to describe what they would do if they were astronauts, artists, teachers, or members of any other profession. You could also invite guests from the community to tell your class about their jobs.

Felíz día de San Valentín

FEBRUARY pages 69–74

Purpose
Children identify direct quotations. Children fill in talk balloons and learn about dialogue.

Strategies for Starting
Discuss Valentine's Day. Ask: *Why do we celebrate Valentine's Day? Whom do you want to show love to on Valentine's Day? How can we show love to people every day?*

Introduce the Book

Read aloud to the class the sample book that you made. You may want to use different voices for the characters so that students can hear the direct quotations. Ask students to guess what you wrote in the talk balloons. Then ask them how they figured this out. Invite students to predict the ending of the book.

Make the Book

Duplicate and pass out pages 69–74 of this book. Either preassemble the books or help children assemble their books. On page 2, invite children to draw a valentine and a rose. Ask students to find the direct quotations on each page by looking for the words inside the dashes. Then have them copy the quotations into the talk balloons to reinforce the concept of using dialogue. Later, give children opportunities to add dialogue to their own writing.

Share the Book

Have children read their books aloud to the class. Ask children to act out the roles of frog, bunny, snail, minnow, and toad. Send the books home for children to read to family members and friends.

Beyond the Book

Invite children to make a valentine card for an animal of their choice. What message do they want to write to the animal? Do they love the stripes on a zebra or the way a cat purrs? Have children write and illustrate their cards, then add them to a Valentine's Day display along with the books they made.

¿De qué tamaño es un duende?

MARCH   pages 75–79

Purpose

Children make size comparisons. Children review comparative adjectives to describe size relationships.

Strategies for Starting

Ask students to choose an object in the classroom. Then assign partners and have them use comparative adjectives to describe the size relationship between the two objects: *más grande, más pequeño, más alto, más bajo, más ancho,* and so on. For example, a student might say, "Mi lápiz es más largo que el borrador de Susana." Discuss leprechauns with the class. Ask: *Does anyone know what a leprechaun is? What do they look like? Do they bring good luck or bad luck? Are they real or imaginary?*

Introduce the Book

Share with the class the book you made as a model. Before you read each page aloud, you may want to ask students to describe the size relationship between the leprechaun and the object. Explain to students that on each page they will choose either "es" or "no es" to complete each sentence.

Make the Book

Duplicate and pass out pages 75–79 of this book. Either preassemble the books or help children assemble their books. Have children determine the size relationship on each page and fill in either "es" or "no es" on the line. On the last page, children can draw themselves either larger or smaller than the leprechaun.

Share the Book

Ask children to read their books aloud with partners, alternating pages. Then send the books home for children to share with family members and friends.

Beyond the Book

Have children use rulers to measure the length and width of various objects. Ask them to record their answers and then compare the sizes of various objects using comparative adjectives.

Los colores de la Tierra

APRIL pages 80–84

Purpose

Students recognize and celebrate the earth's beauty. Children review colors.

Strategies for Starting

Discuss the many beautiful components of the earth: oceans, grass, trees, sand, flowers, rainbows, animals, people, and even the sun, moon, and sky. Have the children consider these elements and describe them using color words. Invite students to think about why we call the earth our home. Ask: *What is a home? Is the earth a home? What makes it a home and who lives in it?*

Introduce the Book

Read aloud to the class the model book you made. Let children suggest colors to fill in the blanks. Point out the pattern of the text and the connections between the illustrations and the words.

Make the Book

Duplicate and pass out pages 80–84 of this book. Either preassemble the books or help children assemble their books. Read through the book together. Invite children to illustrate the pages to correspond to the text. On page 1, have children color each object and then write the color on the line. On pages 2–7, ask children to write the name of an appropriate color on the line. On each page, students can add a picture of themselves or other people enjoying nature.

Share the Book

Read the book aloud together. Send the books home for children to share with family members. After they have returned the books, have children add *The Colors of the Earth* to their personal libraries.

Beyond the Book

- Connect this book with the study of Earth Day (April 22). Discuss how we can care for the earth by picking up litter, recycling, saving energy, planting trees, saving water, avoiding pollution, and caring for wildlife. Engage the class in an environmental project, such as setting up a recycling station in your classroom.

- Have children write letters to their parents to remind them of what they can do to care for the environment. Develop a checklist of things that children and their families can do to help care for the earth. Make copies and send them home with children's letters.

TEACHING TIP: Read books and stories about caring for the earth and appreciating its beauty. Make a class mural showing ways we can protect the environment. Display it in the hallway with written explanations of what students have depicted.

¡Es primavera!

MAY   pages 85–88

Purpose
Children develop expressive language and vocabulary about spring. Children fill in the missing verbs. Children identify the signs of spring.

Strategies for Starting
Have children share their observations of spring. Encourage them to express their ideas using the same pattern as the book, such as "Los pájaros cantan" or "Las lombrices se arrastran."

Introduce the Book
Read aloud the sample book that you made. Emphasize the verbs. Remind children that the illustrations provide clues to the text.

Make the Book
Duplicate and pass out pages 85–88 of this book. Either preassemble the books or help children assemble their books. As a group, brainstorm a list of possible verbs for children to use as they make their books.

Share the Book
Invite children to share their books with partners. Encourage children to write positive comments on the back covers of one another's books. Have them take the books home to read to their families and then bring the books back with responses.

Beyond the Book
Make a bulletin board with the many signs of spring mentioned in the book. Encourage students to watch for signs of spring and record on the bulletin board where and when they take place. Investigate and record the time the sun rises and sets each day, as well as the daily high and low temperature. Challenge students to fill in a bar graph based on this information and then make predictions about tomorrow's weather.

Mi libro de recuerdos

JUNE   pages 89–93

Purpose
Children reflect upon the school year. Children write about special activities and people that shaped the year. Children write about what they learned and enjoyed.

Strategies for Starting
Invite reflection and discussion about the school year. Ask: *Do you remember the first day of the school year? What was it like? How did you feel? What things have you learned since then? What activities have you enjoyed? What people helped to make this a special year? What were the most memorable events of the year? Why?*

Introduce the Book
Read aloud the sample book that you made. Use it as a springboard for further discussion. Encourage students to think of their own favorite memories.

Make the Book

Duplicate and pass out pages 89–93 of this book. Either preassemble the books or help children assemble the books. As children are making their books, ask them questions to help them develop thoughtful, personal recollections. On the cover, invite children to draw people, places, or things that they will remember from the year. Encourage children to draw illustrations that support their writing. The back cover, titled "Autógrafos," is a place for children to sign one another's books.

Share the Book

Have students sit in a circle and pass their books around for others to read and then sign. You may want to invite the people students wrote about in their books, such as administrators, support staff, gym teachers, and art teachers. They will be glad to know that students included them in their memory books. Students will also enjoy asking the guests to sign their books.

Beyond the Book

Invite students to choose one memory from their book—either a person, a special event, or something they learned. Ask them to write more about it and then to paint or draw a large illustration to support what they have written. You can hang these pieces along with the books on a bulletin board display titled "Recordando mi _____ grado."

TEACHING TIP: This memory book is a wonderful way to reflect on and bring closure to the school year. Encourage children to save their memory books as well as all of their Write & Read Books. Emphasize how special it will be for children to look at these books in the future and remember what it was like to be their age.

_____
fecha

Estimados padres:

Una parte de nuestro programa de alfabetización es hacer Write & Read Books, libros para escribir y leer. Los cuentos en estos libros siguen modelos simples iguales a los que usamos para leer en clase. Los niños se sienten muy orgullosos de estos libros y desearían compartirlos con ustedes. Les pedimos por favor que reserven un momento para leer y hablar sobre los libros juntos.

En la contraportada de cada libro encontrarán una página para sus comentarios. Uno o dos comentarios positivos sobre el libro escritos en esta página serían una excelente motivación para su hijo/a. Podrían comentar, por ejemplo, sobre las ideas, las ilustraciones, la ortografía y la presentación del cuento. También podrían mencionar la fluidez y la expresión con que su hijo/a lee, cómo descubre las palabras difíciles, cómo usa las claves del contexto o cómo ha progresado de manera general.

Por favor, devuelvan estos libros con sus comentarios a la escuela antes del _____.

Les agradecemos su participación. Su interés y apoyo son importantes para su nuevo/a lector/a.

                                        Atentamente,

_____

Suenan las campanas

por _____

Comentarios

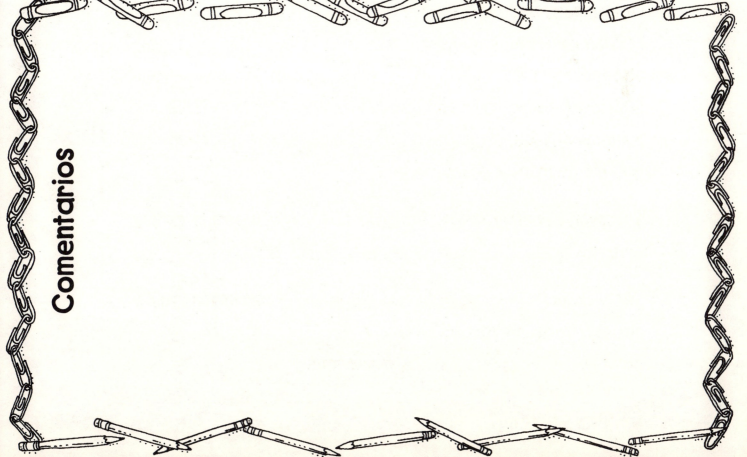

Se acabó el verano,
ya es tiempo de volver a la
_____.

1

Este año estoy en
_____.

2

Lo que más me gusta de la escuela es _____.

4

En la escuela aprendemos a _____ y a _____.

3

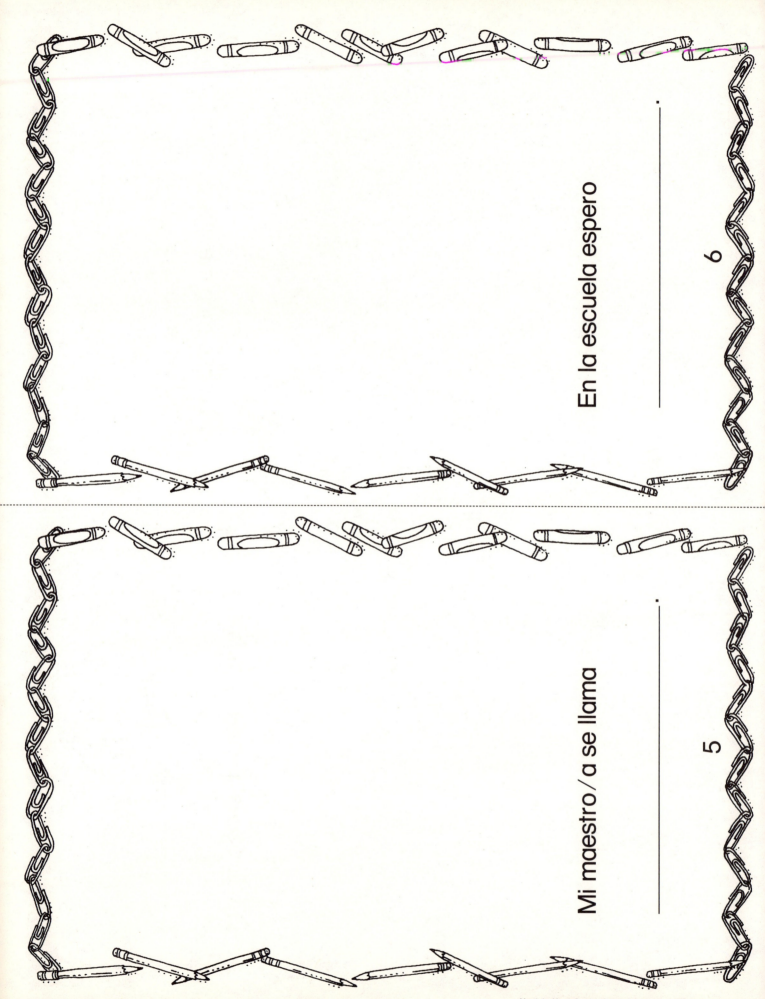

Mi maestro/a se llama _____.

5

En la escuela espero _____.

6

Otoño

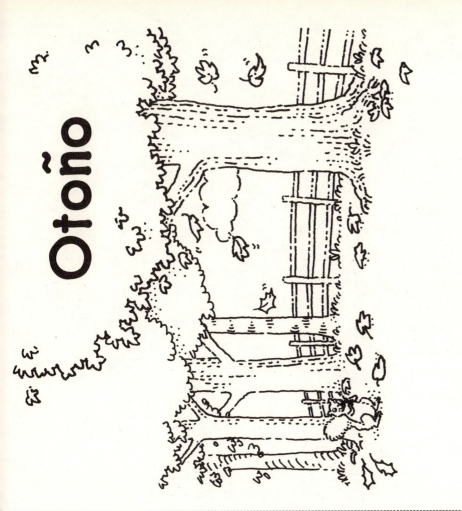

por _____

Comentarios

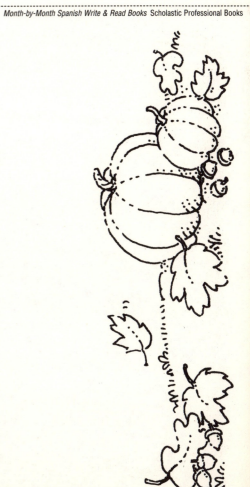

Es otoño y veo cambios a mi alrededor.

Veo caer _____ coloradas de los árboles.

1

Veo _____ en los árboles, listas para cosechar.

2

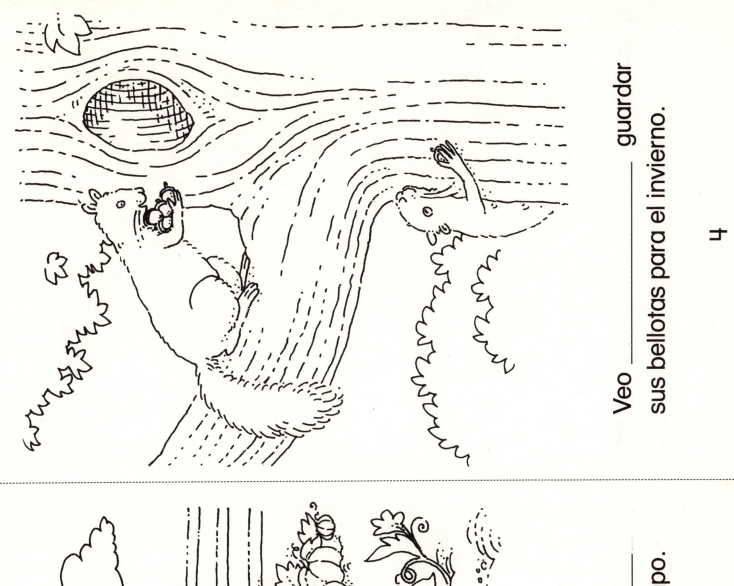

Veo _____ guardar
sus bellotas para el invierno.

4

Veo _____
crecer más gordas en el campo.

3

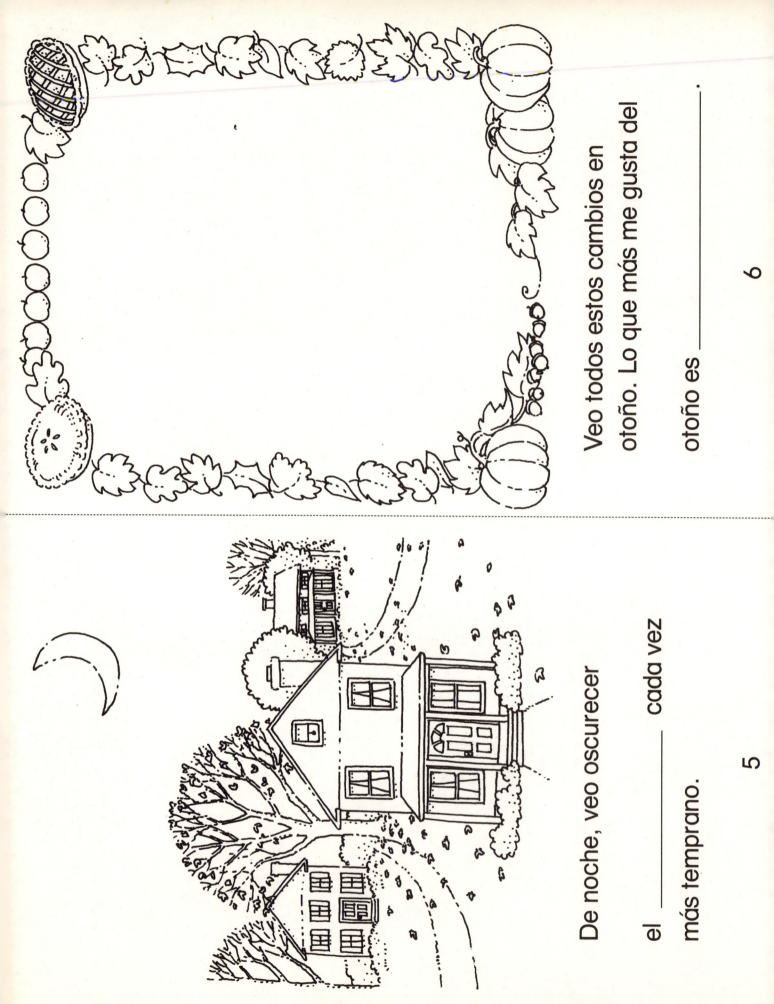

Veo todos estos cambios en otoño. Lo que más me gusta del otoño es _____.

De noche, veo oscurecer el _____ cada vez más temprano.

La cosecha del otoño

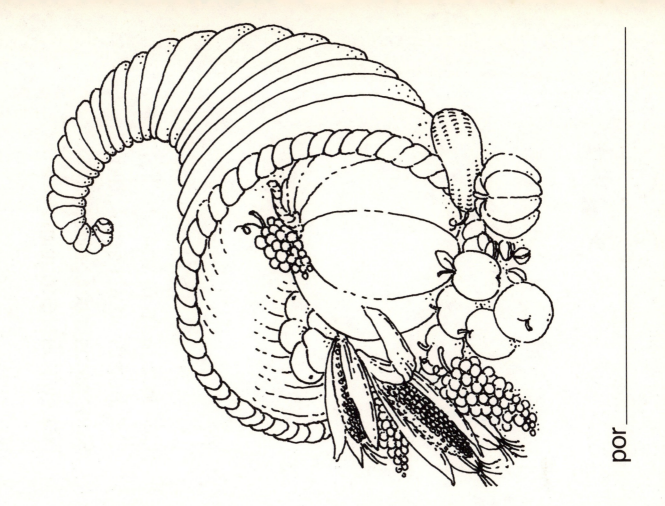

por _____

Month-by-Month Spanish Write & Read Books Scholastic Professional Books

Comentarios

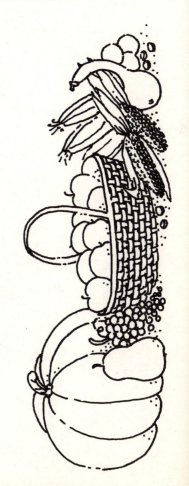

Calabazas en el sembradío,
Calabazas en el sembradío,
Recógelas, recógelas,
Recógelas, recógelas,
Calabazas _____ .

Manzanas en el huerto,
Manzanas en el huerto,
Maduras, maduras,
Maduras, maduras,
Manzanas en el huerto.

Trigo en el campo,
Trigo en el campo,
Córtalo, córtalo,
Córtalo, córtalo,

Trigo _____.

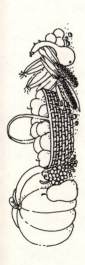

Zanahorias en la tierra,
Zanahorias en la tierra,
Desentiérralas, desentiérralas,
Desentiérralas, desentiérralas,

Zanahorias _____.

Comida en el mercado,
Comida en el mercado,
Sabrosa, sabrosa,
Sabrosa, sabrosa,

Comida _____.

6

Verduras en la huerta,
Verduras en la huerta,
Coséchalas, coséchalas,
Coséchalas, coséchalas,

Verduras _____.

5

Manzanas, manzanas

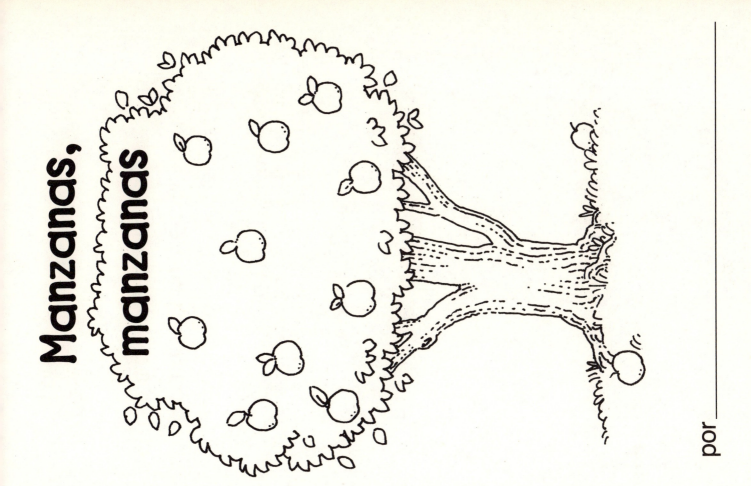

por _____

Comentarios

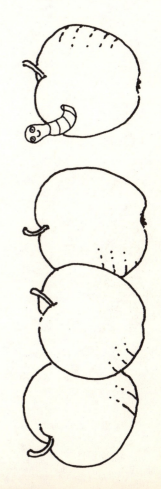

En un árbol hay nueve manzanas, ¿cuántas quedan si una cae de la rama? _____

En un árbol hay diez manzanas, ¿cuántas quedan si una cae de la rama? _____

En un árbol hay ocho manzanas, ¿cuántas quedan si una cae de la rama? _____

En un árbol hay siete manzanas, ¿cuántas quedan si una cae de la rama? _____

En un árbol hay seis manzanas, ¿cuántas quedan si una cae de la rama? _____

En un árbol hay cinco manzanas, ¿cuántas quedan si una cae de la rama? _____

En un árbol hay cuatro manzanas,
¿cuántas quedan si una cae de
la rama? _____

7

En un árbol hay tres manzanas,
¿cuántas quedan si una cae de
la rama? _____

8

En un árbol hay dos manzanas, ¿cuántas quedan si una cae de la rama? _____

9

¡Una manzana sabrosa para mí!

En un árbol hay una manzana, ¿cuántas quedan si una cae de la rama? _____

10

La arañita

por _____

Comentarios

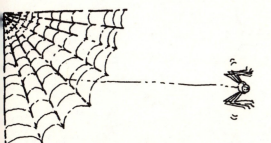

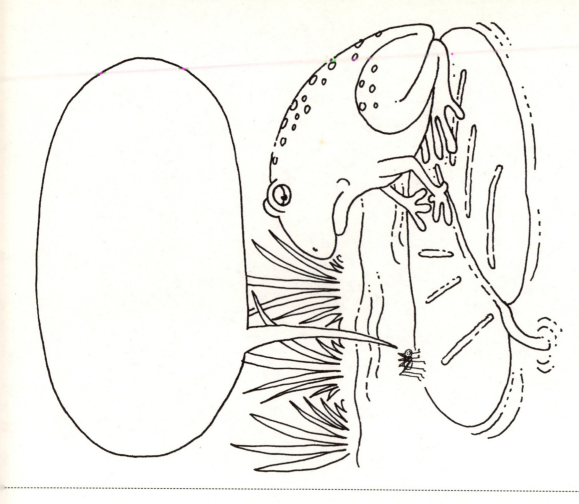

Primero se encontró con una rana ceñuda sentada en una hoja de nenúfar.
—Hola, rana —dijo la arañita.

2

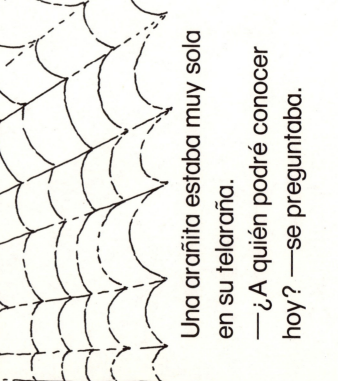

Una arañita estaba muy sola en su telaraña.
—¿A quién podré conocer hoy? —se preguntaba.

1

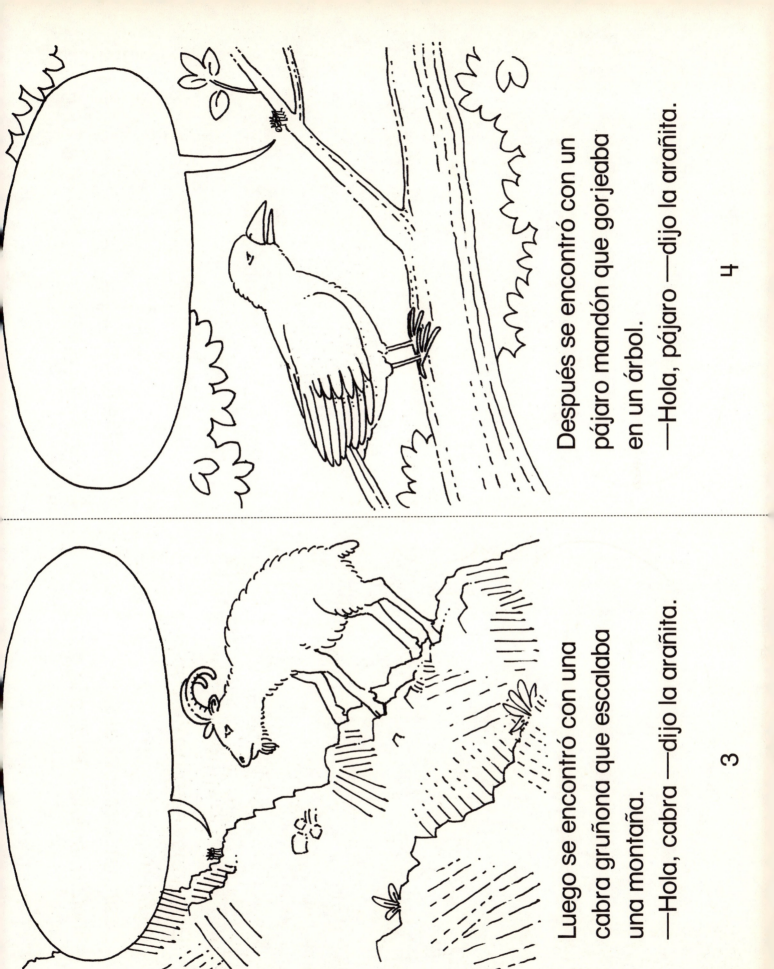

Después se encontró con un
pájaro mandón que gorjeaba
en un árbol.
—Hola, pájaro —dijo la arañita.

4

Luego se encontró con una
cabra gruñona que escalaba
una montaña.
—Hola, cabra —dijo la arañita.

3

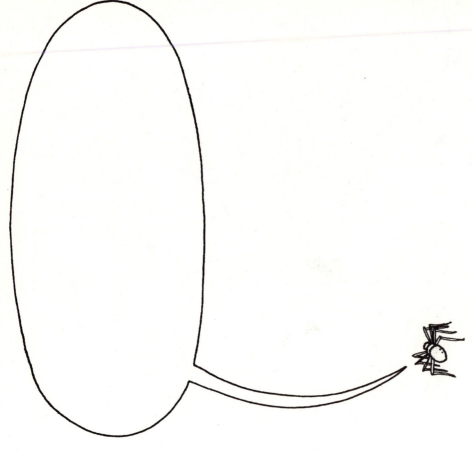

Por fin, se encontró con un niño alegre leyendo un libro sobre una araña.

—Hola, ___ESCRIBE TU NOMBRE AQUÍ___ —dijo la arañita—. ¡Vamos a jugar!

6

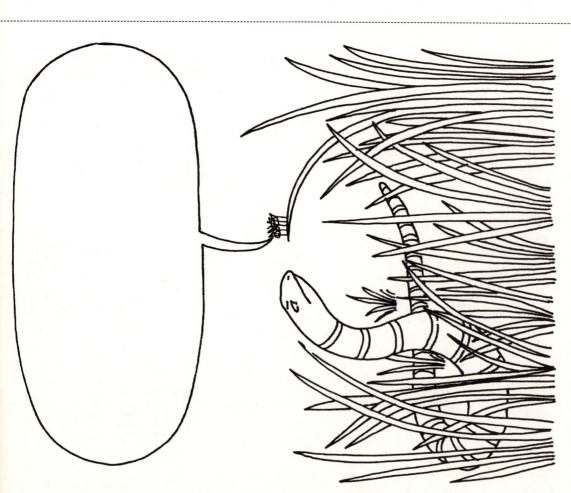

Entonces se encontró con una culebra silenciosa que se deslizaba por el pasto.

—Hola, culebra —dijo la arañita.

5

Doy gracias

por _____

Comentarios

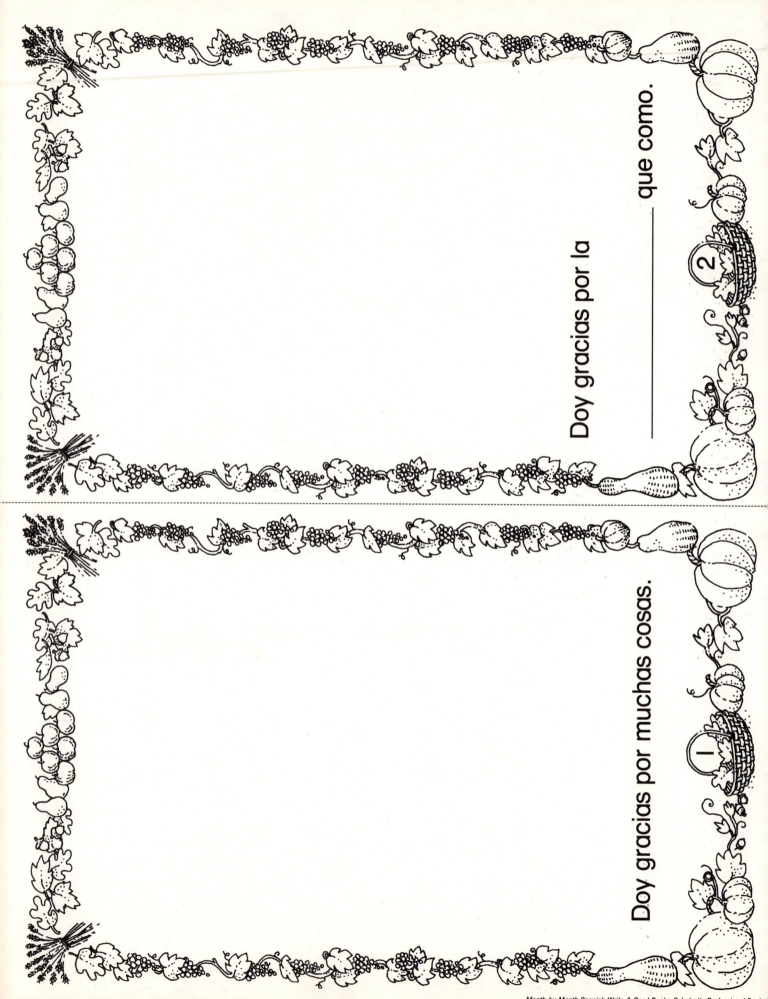

Doy gracias por _____ en que vivo.

4

Doy gracias por la _____ que llevo puesta.

3

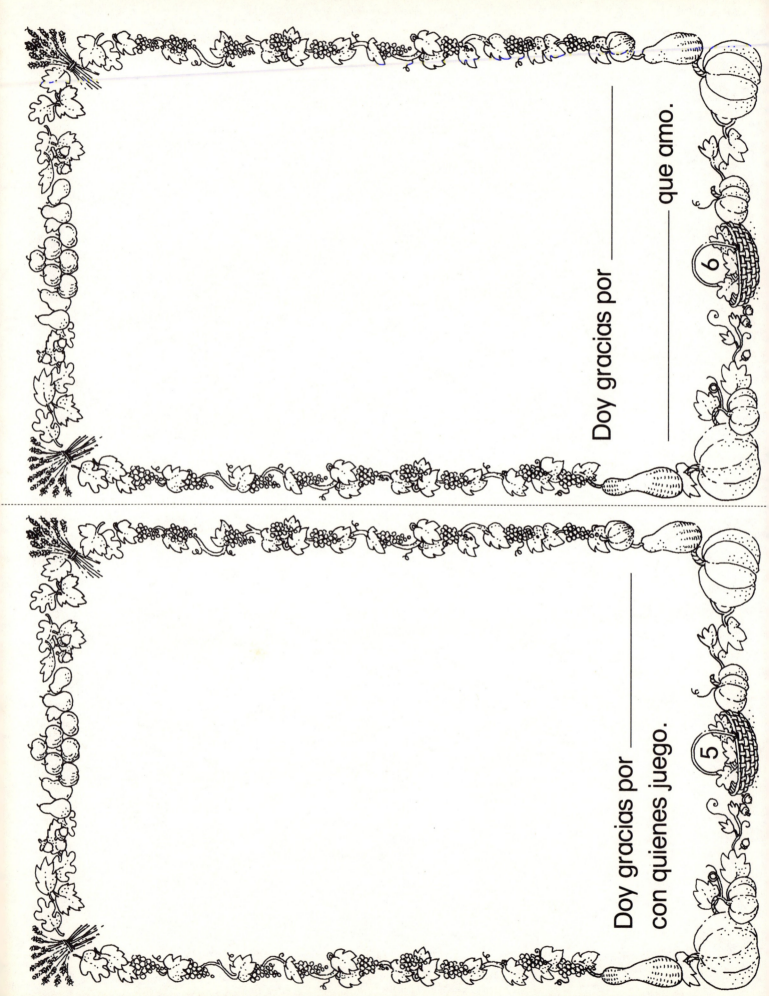

Doy gracias por _____ con quienes juego.

5

Doy gracias por _____ que amo.

6

Doy gracias por _____
que veo afuera.

7

Doy gracias por _____
_____.

8

Una fría mañana de nieve

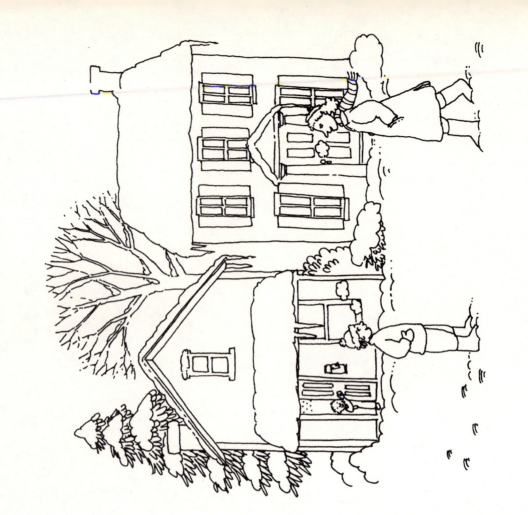

por _____

Comentarios

caer ———— lindos copos de nieve,

2

Una fría mañana de nieve, de camino a la escuela vi...

1

vagar ___ nubes grises,

4

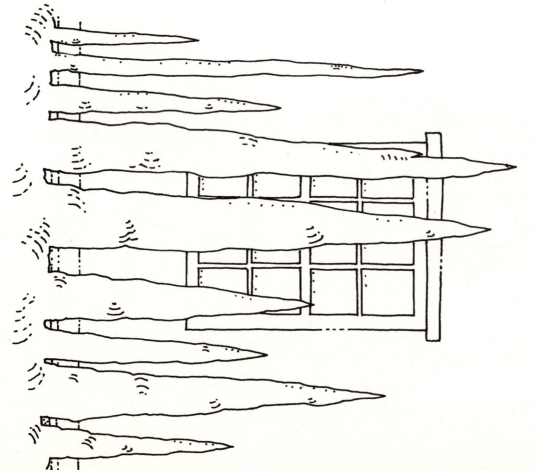

___ bonitos
carámbanos colgando,

3

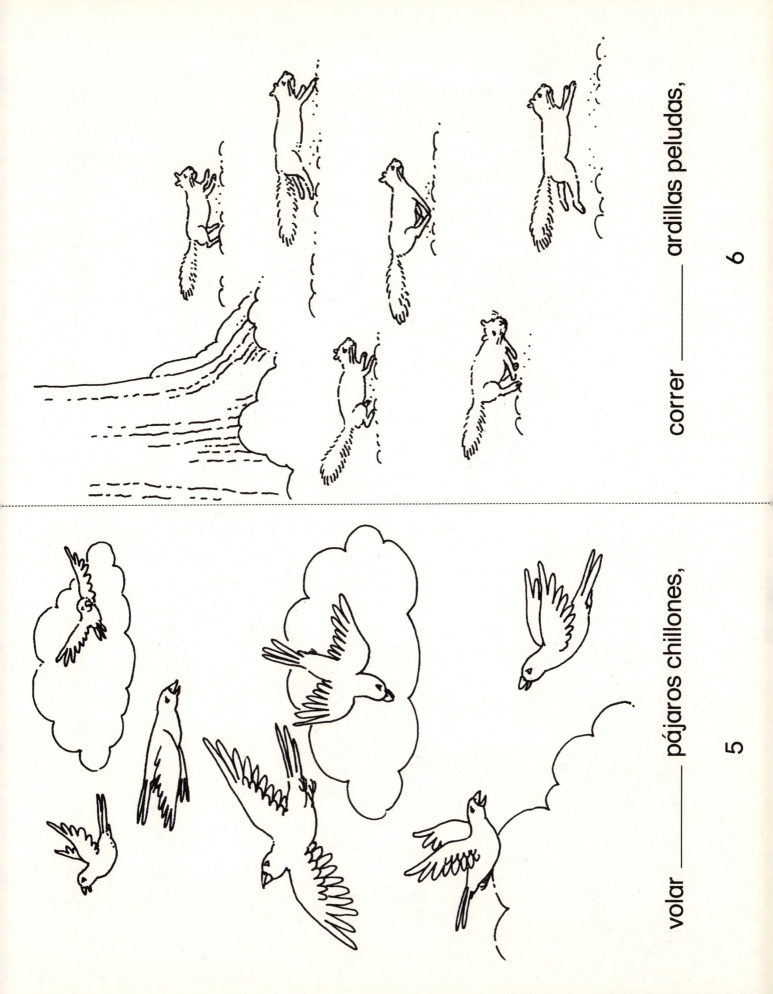

_____ correr _____ ardillas peludas,

6

_____ volar _____ pájaros chillones,

5

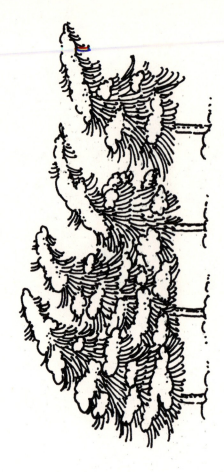

_____ árboles altos inclinarse,

8

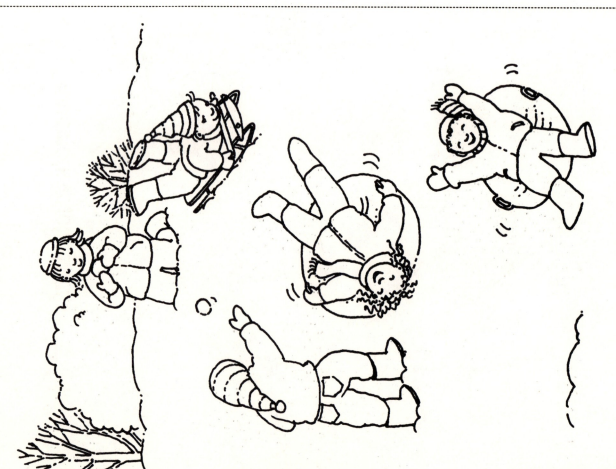

jugar _____ niños felices,

7

_____ palas quitar la nieve,

9

_____ quitanieves avanzar.

10

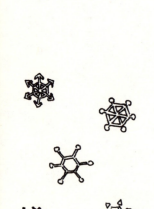

Vi todas esas cosas una fría mañana de nieve. ¡Es invierno!

12

¡Y _____ muñeco de nieve sonriendo!

11

Cómo hacer un muñeco de nieve

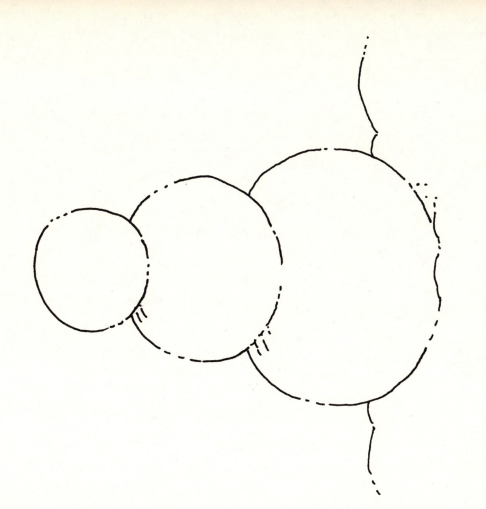

por _____

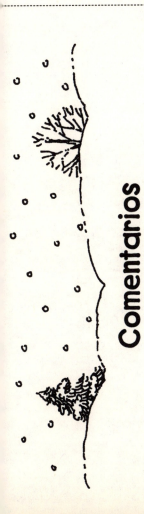

Comentarios

Primero hice _____ pelotas de nieve y las puse una encima de la otra.

2

Así es como hice mi muñeco de nieve.

1

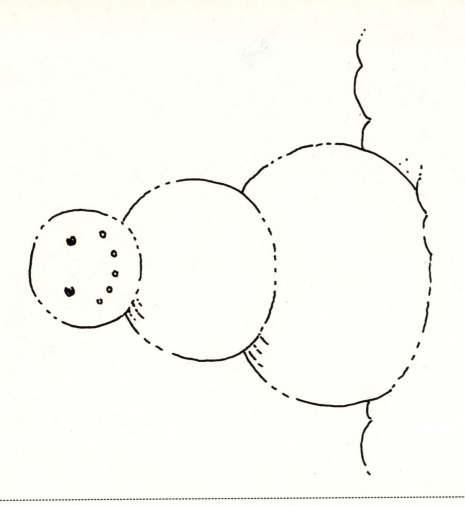

Después, le puse _____ caramelitos para la boca.

4

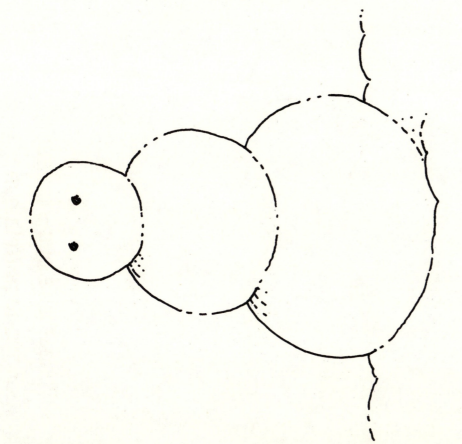

Después, le puse _____ ojos de carbón.

3

Después, le puse _____ zanahoria para la nariz.

5

Después, le puse _____ ramas para los brazos.

6

Por fin, le puse una bufanda y un sombrero.
Llamé a mi muñeco de nieve _____.

8

Después, le puse _____ piedritas para los botones de la panza.

7

¡Es divertido contar hasta cien!

por _____

Comentarios

1 2 3 4 5 6 7 8 9 10 11 12 13 14 15 16 17 18 19 **20** 21 22 23 24 25 26 27 28 29 **30** 31 32 33 34 35 36 37 38 39 **40** 41 42 43 44 45 46 47 48 49 **50** 51 52 53 54 55 56 57 58 59 **60** 61 62 63 64 65 66 67 68 69 **70** 71 72 73 74 75 76 77 78 79 **80** 81 82 83 84 85 86 87 88 89 **90** 91 92 93 94 95 96 97 98 99 **100**

Aquí hay diez cosas calientes.

2

Diez por diez es divertido contar.
¡Cien es una gran cantidad!

1

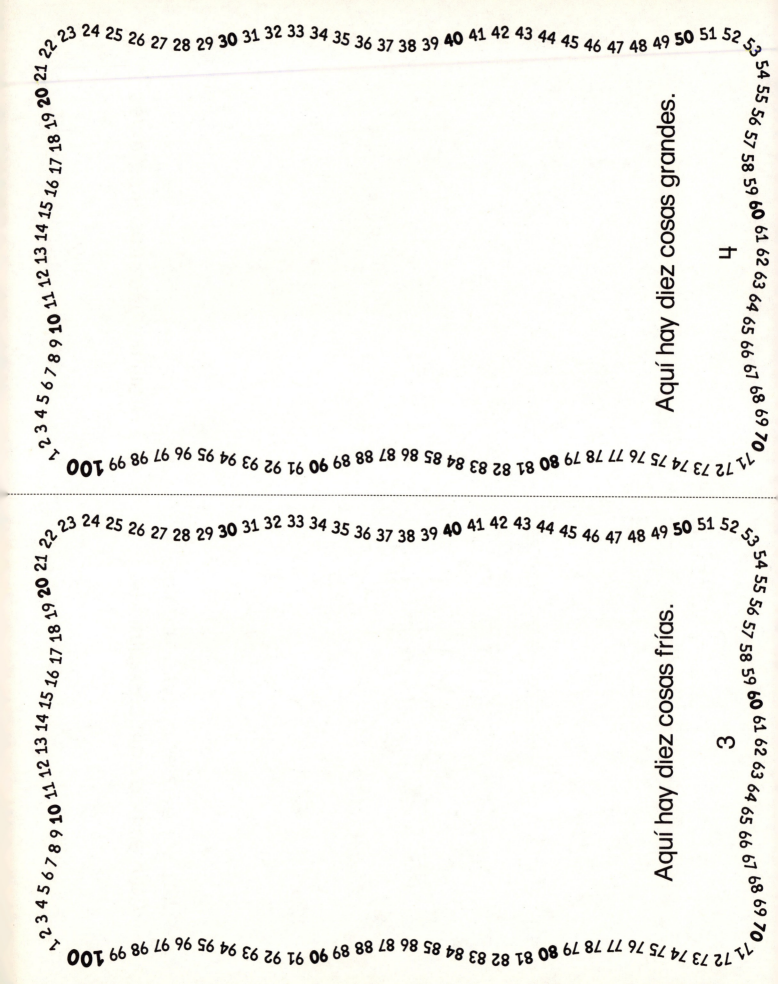

Frame with numbers 1–100 around the border:

Aquí hay diez cosas redondas.

6

Aquí hay diez cosas pequeñas.

5

Month-by-Month Spanish Write & Read Books Scholastic Professional Books

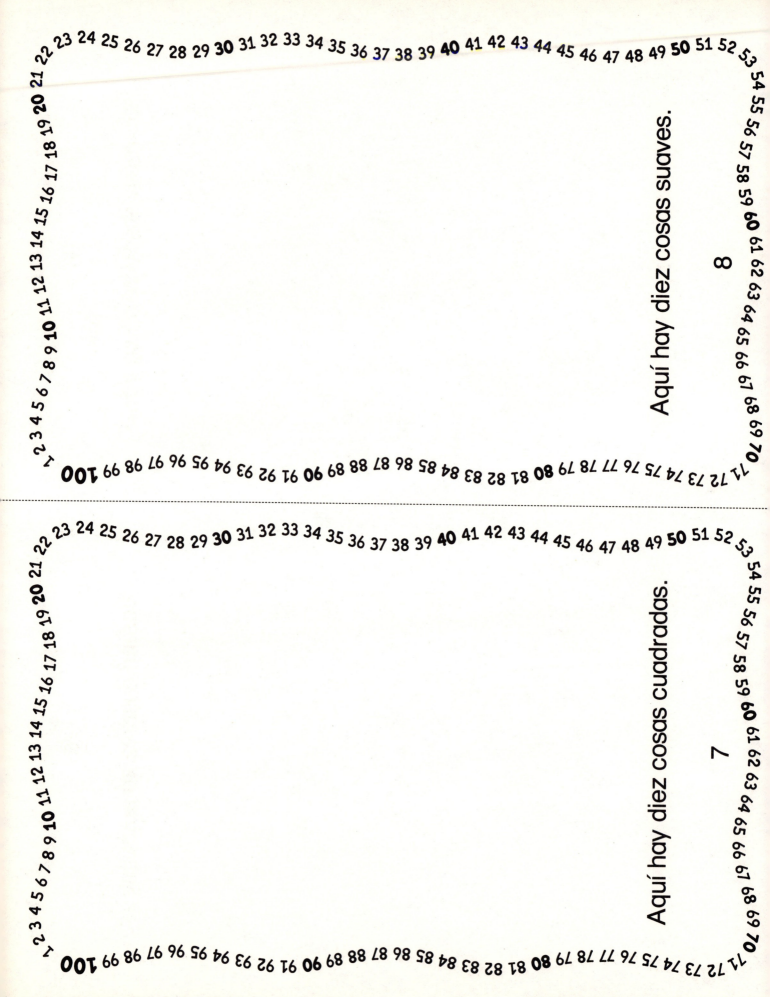

1 2 3 4 5 6 7 8 9 10 11 12 13 14 15 16 17 18 19 20 21 22 23 24 25 26 27 28 29 30 31 32 33 34 35 36 37 38 39 40 41 42 43 44 45 46 47 48 49 50 51 52 53 54 55 56 57 58 59 60 61 62 63 64 65 66 67 68 69 70 71 72 73 74 75 76 77 78 79 80 81 82 83 84 85 86 87 88 89 90 91 92 93 94 95 96 97 98 99 100

Aquí hay diez cosas ruidosas.

10

---

1 2 3 4 5 6 7 8 9 10 11 12 13 14 15 16 17 18 19 20 21 22 23 24 25 26 27 28 29 30 31 32 33 34 35 36 37 38 39 40 41 42 43 44 45 46 47 48 49 50 51 52 53 54 55 56 57 58 59 60 61 62 63 64 65 66 67 68 69 70 71 72 73 74 75 76 77 78 79 80 81 82 83 84 85 86 87 88 89 90 91 92 93 94 95 96 97 98 99 100

Aquí hay diez cosas duras.

9

Diez por diez es divertido contar.
¡Cien es una gran cantidad!

12

Aquí hay diez cosas silenciosas.

11

Si yo fuera presidente

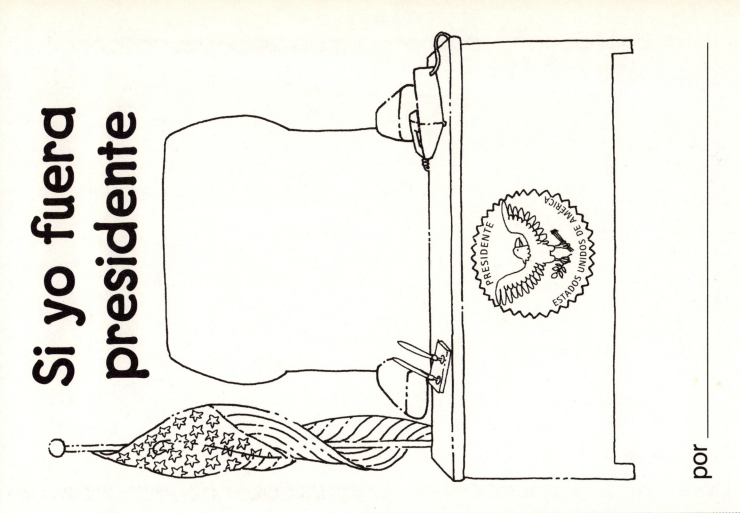

por _____

Comentarios

Si yo fuera presidente, la primera cosa que haría es _____.

1

Si yo fuera presidente, comería _____.

2

Si yo fuera presidente, tendría una mascota llamada _____.

4

Si yo fuera presidente, viajaría a _____.

3

Si yo fuera presidente, ayudaría a _____.

6

Si yo fuera presidente, haría una ley que _____.

5

Feliz día de San Valentín

por _____

Comentarios

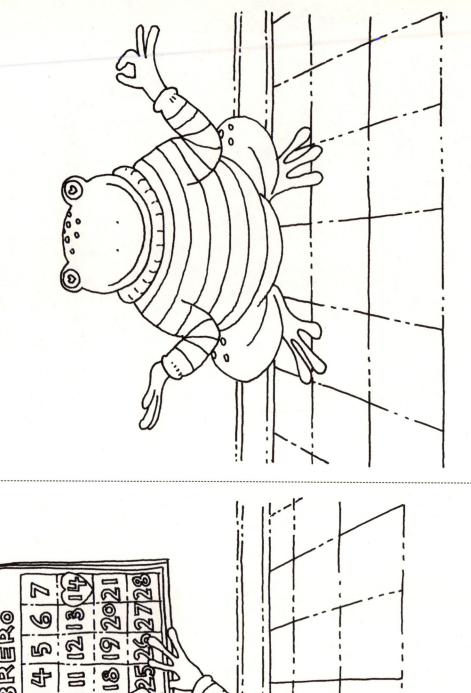

Había una vez un sapo de corazón generoso. ¿Quién sería su amiga el día de San Valentín?

1

El sapo hizo una hermosa tarjeta roja y cortó una rosa roja. ¿A quién se la daría el día de San Valentín?

2

En eso Carmen Coneja llegó saltando.
—¿Quieres ser mi amiga? —le preguntó.

—Yo no —dijo Carmen Coneja.
—Mi amigo es el oso.
Y se fue saltando.

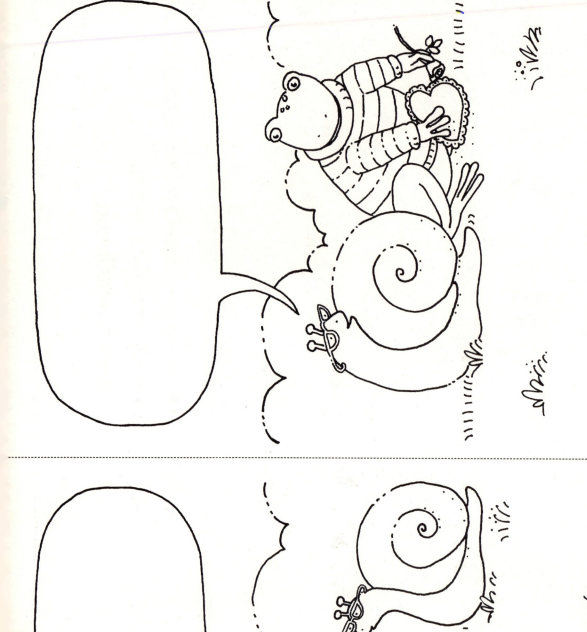

En eso Clara Caracol llegó arrastrándose.
—¿Quieres ser mi amiga? —le preguntó.

—Yo no —dijo Clara Caracol.
—Mi amigo es el ratón.
Y se fue arrastrando.

—Yo no —dijo Pepita Pececillo.
—Mi amigo es el pato.
Y se fue nadando.

8

En eso llegó nadando Pepita Pececillo.
—¿Quieres ser mi amiga? —le preguntó.

7

El sapo llegó saltando a su casa
y allí lo esperaba Rita Rana.
Ella tenía una hermosa tarjeta y
una rosa roja.

—¿Quieres ser mi amigo?
—le preguntó.
—Por supuesto —dijo el sapo—.
¡Feliz día de San Valentín!

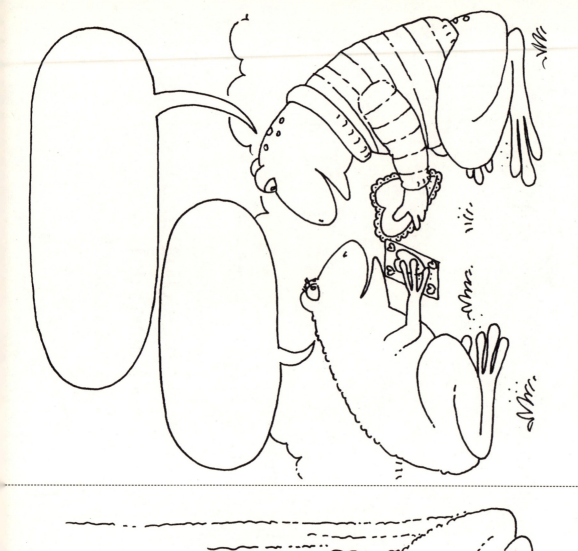

¿De qué tamaño es un duende?

por _____

Comentarios

Un duende _____ es / no es
más grande que una manzana.

2

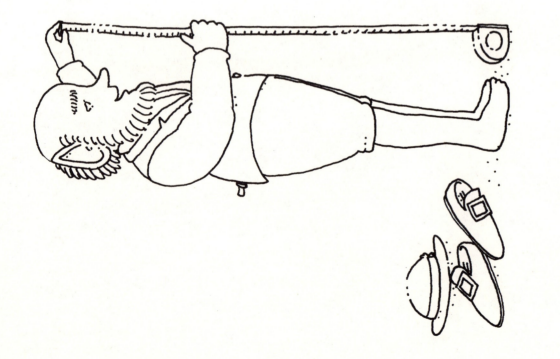

¿De qué tamaño crees
que es un duende?

1

Un duende ___es / no es___
más alto que un poste de farol.

4

Un duende ___es / no es___
más grande que una ballena.

3

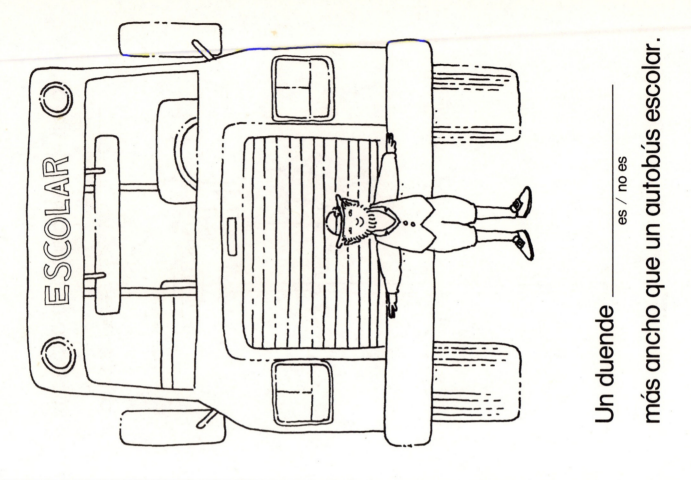

Un duende _____ es / no es

más ancho que un autobús escolar.

Un duende _____ es / no es

más alto que un clavo.

Un duende ____ es / no es ____ más ancho que un caracol.

7

Un duende ____ es / no es ____ más grande que yo.
¡Mira el dibujo y verás!

8

Los colores de la Tierra

por _____

Month-by-Month Spanish Write & Read Books Scholastic Professional Books

Comentarios

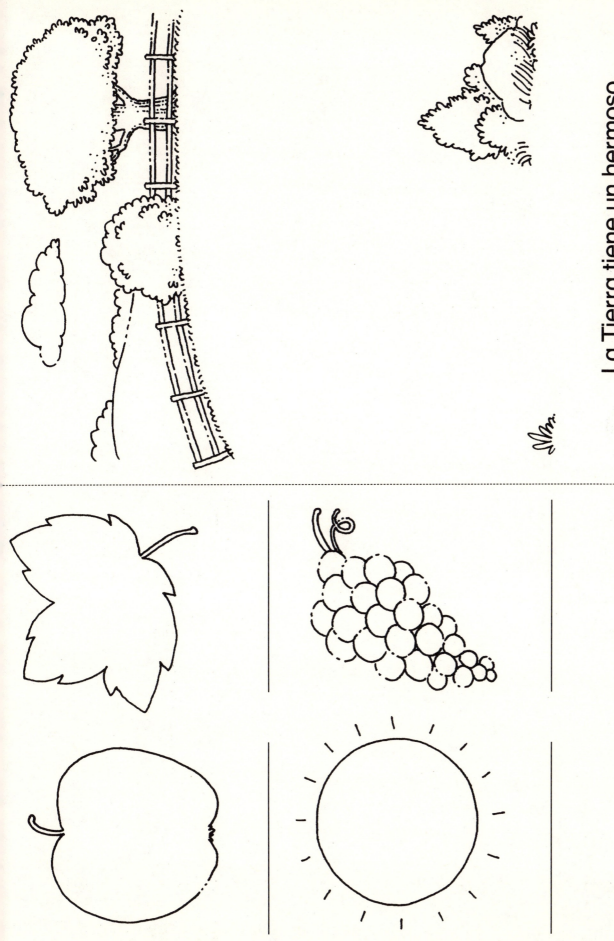

La Tierra tiene un hermoso

pasto _____.

2

La Tierra tiene muchos colores hermosos. ¿Puedes nombrarlos?

1

La Tierra tiene un hermoso _____.
cielo

3

La Tierra tiene hermosas _____.
calabazas

4

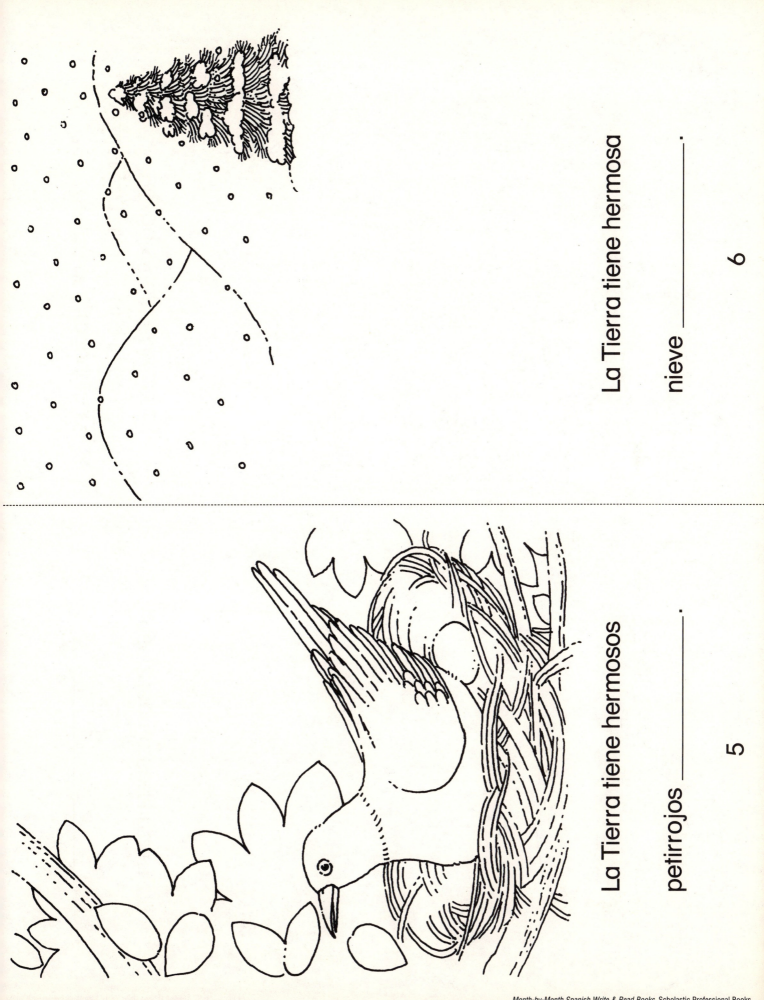

La Tierra tiene hermosa

nieve _____.

6

La Tierra tiene hermosos

petirrojos _____.

5

Todos los colores hacen hermosa a la Tierra. La Tierra es mi hogar y la quiero.

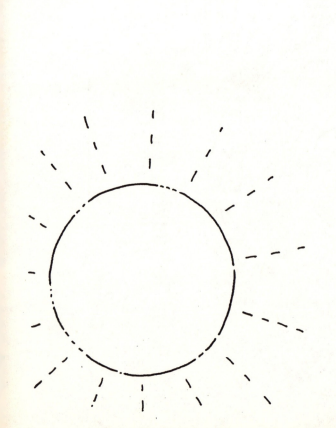

La Tierra tiene un hermoso

Sol _____ .

¡Es primavera!

por _____

Comentarios

Las flores brotan.

2

¡Es primavera! ¡Mira lo que pasa por todas partes!

1

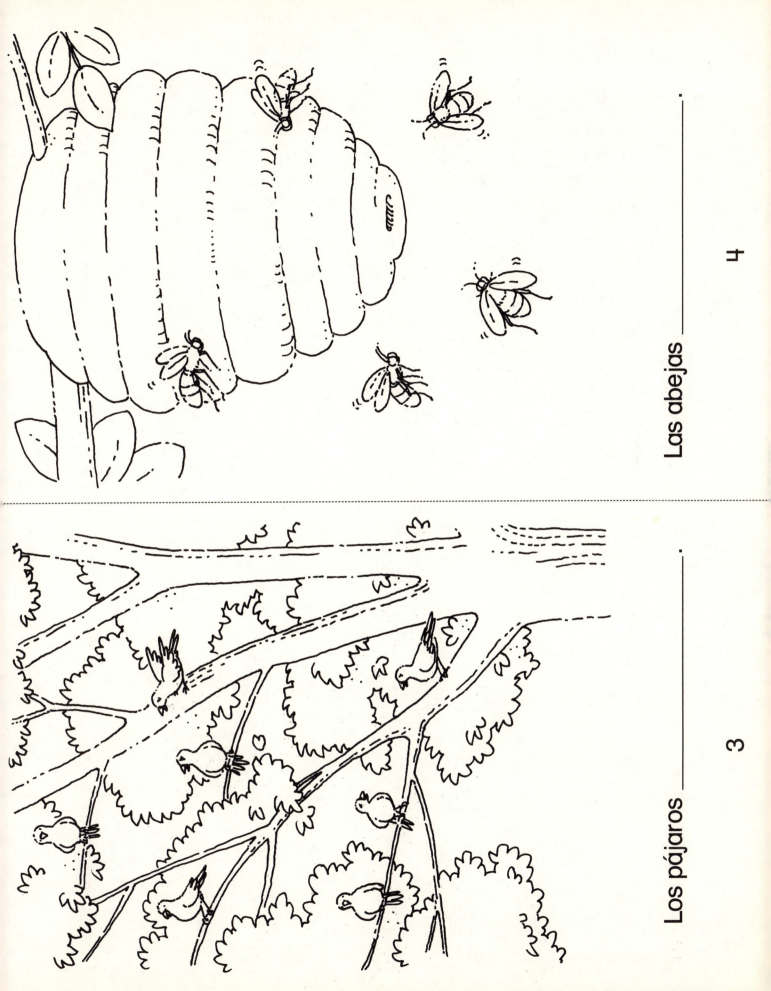

Las abejas _____. 4

Los pájaros _____. 3

Los niños _____.

¡Es primavera!

Mi libro de recuerdos

por _____

Autógrafos

Mi maestro/a se llamaba _____.

2

Mi primer día en la _____ fue _____.

1

Aprendí muchas cosas nuevas.

Aprendí a _____

y a _____.

3

Mi actividad favorita era

_____.

4

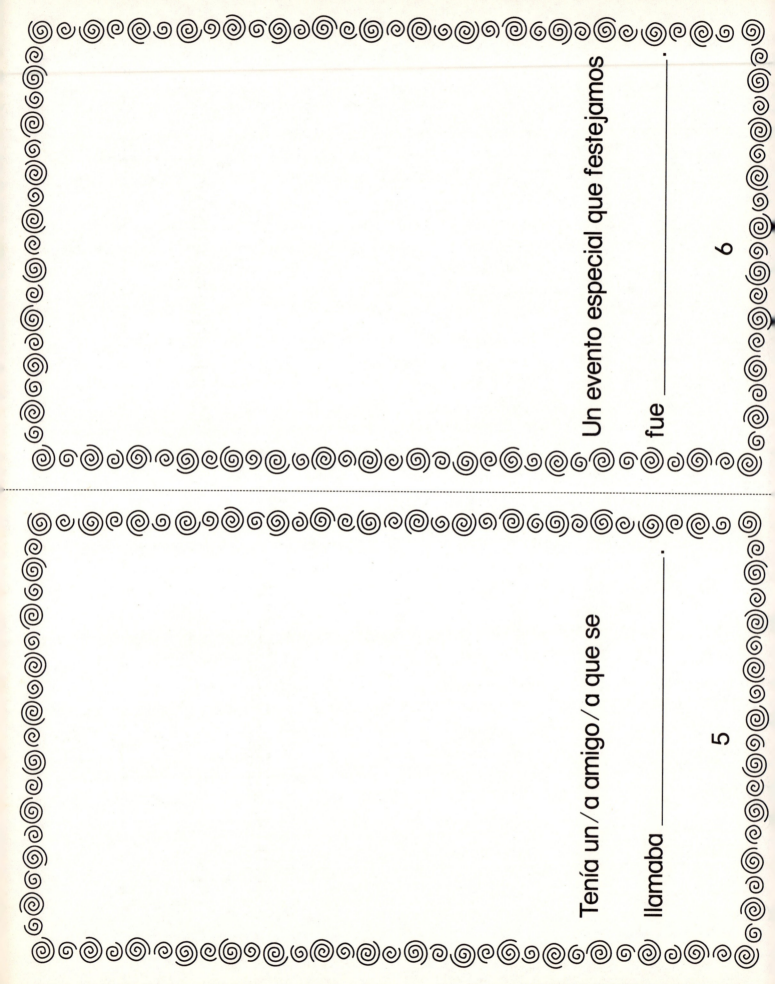

Tenía un/a amigo/a que se llamaba _____.

5

Un evento especial que festejamos fue _____.

6

Algunos de los maestros y los ayudantes especiales eran _____.

¡Tuvimos un fantástico año en la _____!

Este es el retrato de _____.

Sobre el autor

Este libro fue hecho por _____.

_____ tiene _____ años de edad. A _____

le gusta _____, y _____.

Otros libros por este autor son _____

_____.

por _____

Comentarios

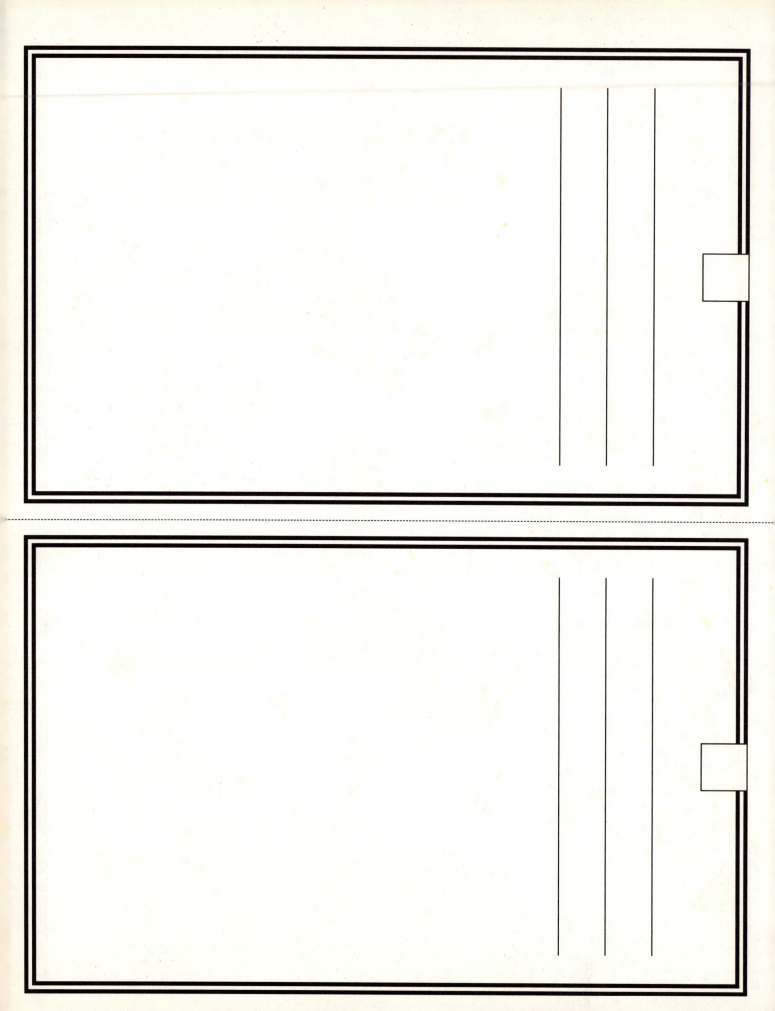